572.4   Parker, Victoria.
Par   Food

MAR 1 3

APR 0 2 2010

MAY 2 1 2010

NOV

APR 2 2 2013

OCT - 9 2014

FEB 1 7 2016

MAR 4 2016

SEP 2 9 2016

NOV

JAN - 7 2019

K+P - J

AR 1.8
0.5 pts

What Living Things Need

Food

Vic Parker

Heinemann Library
Chicago, Illinois

© 2006 Heinemann Library
a division of Reed Elsevier Inc.
Chicago, Illinois

Customer Service   888-454-2279

Visit our website at www.heinemannraintree.com

Printed and bound in China by South China Printing Company Limited
Photo research by Ruth Blair and Andrea Sadler

10 09 08 07 06
10 9 8 7 6 5 4 3 2 1

Library of Congress Cataloging-in-Publication Data

Parker, Victoria.
  Food / Vic Parker.
      p. cm. -- (What living things need)
Includes bibliographical references and index.
ISBN 1-4034-7884-8 (lib. bdg. : alk. paper) -- ISBN 1-4034-7890-2 (pbk. : alk. paper)
1. Animals--Food--Juvenile literature. 2. Food--Juvenile literature. I. Title. II. Series.
  QL756.5.P38 2006
  572'.4--dc22
                                        2005025126

Acknowledgments
The author and publishers are grateful to the following for permission to reproduce copyright material: Alamy p. **5**; Corbis pp. **6** (Ariel Skelley), **12**, **14**, **19**, **23** (farm), back cover (orange); FLPA pp. **15** (E & D Hosking), **16** (B. Borrell Casals), **17** (Foto Natura Stock), **18** (Gerard Lacz), **23** (insects, B. Borrell Casals), **23** (bamboo, Gerard Lacz), back cover (ladybird, B. Borrell Casals); Getty Images pp. **7** (Taxi), **20** (Photodisc), **22** (child, Digital Vision), **22** (bone, Photodisc), **22** (dog, Photodisc), **22** (rabbit, Photodisc); Harcourt Education Ltd pp. **13**, **23** (market); Harcourt Education Ltd (cornflakes, Tudor Photography) p. **22**; KPT Power Photos p. **22** (carrot); NHPA (A.N.T. Photo Library) p. **21**; Photolibrary.com pp. **4**, **11**; Powerstock (Maureen Lawrence) pp. **8**, **23** (energy); TopFoto pp. **9** (Bob Daemmrich, The Image Works), **10** (Esbin-Anderson, The Image Works).

Cover photograph reproduced with permission of Corbis.

Every effort has been made to contact copyright holders of any material reproduced in this book. Any omissions will be rectified in subsequent printings if notice is given to the publisher.

Many thanks to the teachers, library media specialists, reading instructors, and educational consultants who have helped develop the Read and Learn/Lee y aprende brand.

Contents

Some words are shown in bold, **like this**. You can find them in the picture glossary on page 23.

What Is a Living Thing?

Living things are things that grow.

People, animals, and plants are living things.

Which things in this picture are living and which are not?

What Is Food?

Food is everything that we
eat and drink.

Living things eat different types
of food.

Why Do We Need Food?

We need food to live.

Food gives us **energy** to talk, think, and move.

Food helps us to grow.

If we do not eat food, we get
hungry and feel sick.

What Food Do We Need?

Every day we need to eat different types of food.

We need to eat fruit and vegetables because they are good for us.

If we eat too much food, we feel sick!

Where Does Our Food Come From?

Much of the food we eat comes from **farms**.

Some food is made into meals at factories.

We go to stores and **markets** to
buy food.

How Do Animals Get Their Food?

Some animals find their food.

This giraffe is looking for tasty leaves.

Some animals hunt for food.

This owl has caught a mouse
to eat.

What Do Animals Eat?

Some animals eat other animals for food.

This ladybug eats **insects** like this fly.

Some animals eat plants as well as animals.

These fish eat plants and insects.

Do All Animals Eat Other Animals?

Some animals only eat plants.
They do not eat other animals.

This panda eats **bamboo** plants.

Horses only eat plants, too.

They eat grass and hay.
Hay is dried grass.

How Do Plants Get Food?

Plants make their own food.

Plants mix sunlight, air, and water in their leaves to make food.

This plant makes its own food, but it also eats **insects**!

It is called a Venus flytrap.

Can You Guess?

carrot

dog

bone

child

cereal

rabbit

Can you match these foods with the living things that eat them?

Glossary

 **bamboo** a leafy plant which has long, strong stems

 **energy** the ability to move and do things

 **farm** place where plants are grown and animals are raised for food

 **insects** animals with six legs, such as beetles

 **market** a place where people bring things to sell

Index

Note to Parents and Teachers

Reading nonfiction texts for information is an important part of a child's literacy development. Readers can be encouraged to ask simple questions and then use the text to find the answers. Most chapters in this book begin with a question. Read the questions together. Look at the pictures. Talk about what the answer might be. Then read the text to find out if your predictions were correct. To develop readers' enquiry skills, encourage them to think of other questions they might ask about the topic. Discuss where you could find the answers. Assist children in using the contents page, picture glossary and index to practise research skills and new vocabulary.